Moctezuma
Aztec Ruler

Wendy Conklin, M.A.

Publishing Credits

Content Consultant
Heather Teague

Associate Editor
Christina Hill, M.A.

Assistant Editor
Torrey Maloof

Editorial Assistants
Deborah Buchanan
Kathryn R. Kiley
Judy Tan

Editorial Director
Emily R. Smith, M.A.Ed.

Editor-in-Chief
Sharon Coan, M.S.Ed.

Editorial Manager
Gisela Lee, M.A.

Creative Director
Lee Aucoin

Cover Designer
Lesley Palmer

Designers
Deb Brown
Zac Calbert
Amy Couch
Robin Erickson
Neri Garcia

Publisher
Rachelle Cracchiolo, M.S.Ed.

Teacher Created Materials
5301 Oceanus Drive
Huntington Beach, CA 92649
http://www.tcmpub.com
ISBN 978-0-7439-0457-5
© 2007 Teacher Created Materials, Inc.

Table of Contents

Meet Moctezuma II

There are many famous rulers from the past. Some of these rulers lived in an area called Mesoamerica (meh-zo-uh-MER-ih-kuh). One great ruler was named Moctezuma II (mawk-tuh-ZOO-muh). He ruled one of the most powerful empires at the time. This empire was in Mexico and his people were the Aztecs (AZ-teks).

Moctezuma II

The Aztecs had lived there just a short time when Moctezuma II became king. This was in 1502. They built their city in the middle of a lake. It had all the things a major city needed. Their beliefs in the gods ruled their daily actions. To please these gods, they built temples that looked like pyramids.

The Aztecs were expert warriors and knew how to win in battle. Most of central Mexico was under their rule. They won each battle, and it looked as though no one could defeat them. Then, in 1519, some unexpected Spanish guests showed up. And, it all came to an end.

Mexico today ▶

AZTEC CIVILIZATION 1325–1521

Tuxpan

Gulf of Mexico

ochtitlan

Coatzacoalcos

AZTEC EMPIRE

Huaxyacac

Tehuantepec

Aztec Ruins Today

To this day, many of the Aztec sites are hidden. Some still lay under Mexico City. Others are slowly being uncovered.

Two Moctezumas?

Moctezuma II's father was Moctezuma I. Moctezuma I is not very well known. So, Moctezuma II is usually called just Moctezuma.

Aztec Capital

The Aztec capital city was located where Mexico City is today.

Moctezuma, the Priest

As a child, Moctezuma went to a special school called a *calmecac* (kahl-MEH-kahk). This school taught boys how to be priests. He studied the calendar, religion, poetry, songs, speech, writing, history, law, and war. When he grew up, Moctezuma ran the school.

Aztec priests had important jobs. The priests took care of the temples. They believed in many gods and offered them **sacrifices** (SAK-ruh-fice-ez). Thousands of these sacrifices were people. The Aztecs felt it was an honor to be sacrificed.

These temples were built ▼ before the Aztecs. But, the Aztecs also ruled the area.

Other Aztec Schools

Mostly children from nobility went to the *calmecac*. Commoners attended a school called a *telpochcalli* (tel-pohch-KAH-gee). Elders ran these schools and taught warfare, trade skills, religion, and history.

Priestesses

The Aztecs also set up temple schools for girls from noble families. Here, they could learn how to serve the community as priestesses.

Military School

Some boys attended a special military school where they learned only the art of war.

▲ This is the Wall of Skulls. It is where Aztecs placed the skulls of people who were sacrificed.

Priests studied **astronomy** (uhs-TRAWN-uh-mee) to see if the gods were happy with them. It was important to make these gods happy. The Aztecs thought that the sky held messages from the gods. Moctezuma learned how to read the sky. Many Aztecs thought he was a wise man.

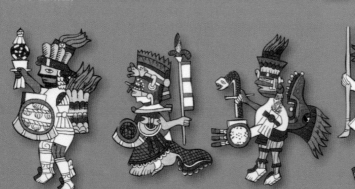

◄ Aztec gods

7

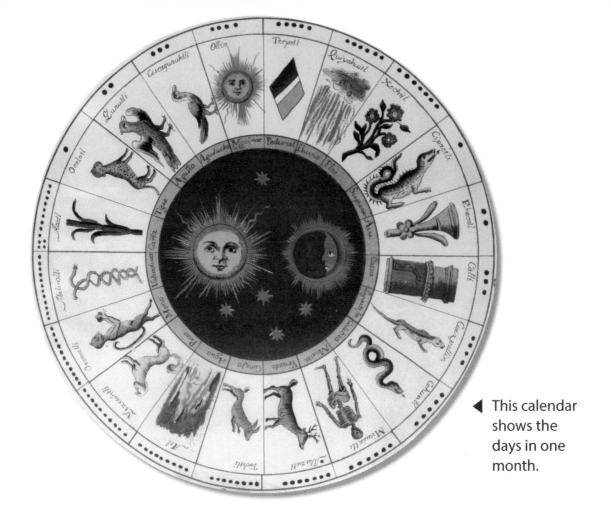

This calendar shows the days in one month.

Reading a Calendar

Another group of people in Mesoamerica were the Mayas. The Mayas created very detailed calendars. The Mayas used the calendars to make big decisions like when to go to war. These calendars were the most advanced of any in the world at the time.

The Aztec calendar was much like the one used by the Mayas. It had both lucky and unlucky days. The *calmecac* trained the future priests to read this calendar. Moctezuma knew how to do this.

The Aztec calendar had 18 months. Each month had 20 days. At the end of this cycle, five unlucky days remained. They believed the unlucky forces roamed freely at this time.

Each month of the calendar year had its own **rituals** (RICH-u-wuhlz). Some months honored battles. Other months showed Aztecs when to plant crops, build homes, or honor the dead.

▼ You can see glyphs on the Calendar Stone.

Serving in the Army

The Aztecs were almost always at war. They had to have a fierce army. At one time, Moctezuma was a general in this army. He knew how to fight and lead men. The Aztecs conquered the groups living nearby.

Conquered groups paid taxes to the Aztecs. Often, this tax was paid in **cacao** (kuh-KOW) beans. Moctezuma brought in 50 thousand pounds (22,700 kg) of beans each year during his **reign** (RAIN). At times, they offered these beans as sacrifices to the gods.

The most skilled soldiers were part of two groups called the Eagle Warriors and the Jaguar Warriors. These men were born into noble families. They were very brave. To be one of these warriors, the men had to prove themselves. First, they fought in hand-to-hand combat. Then, they had to capture others in battle.

▲ This piece of art shows a Jaguar Warrior. It can also be played to make music.

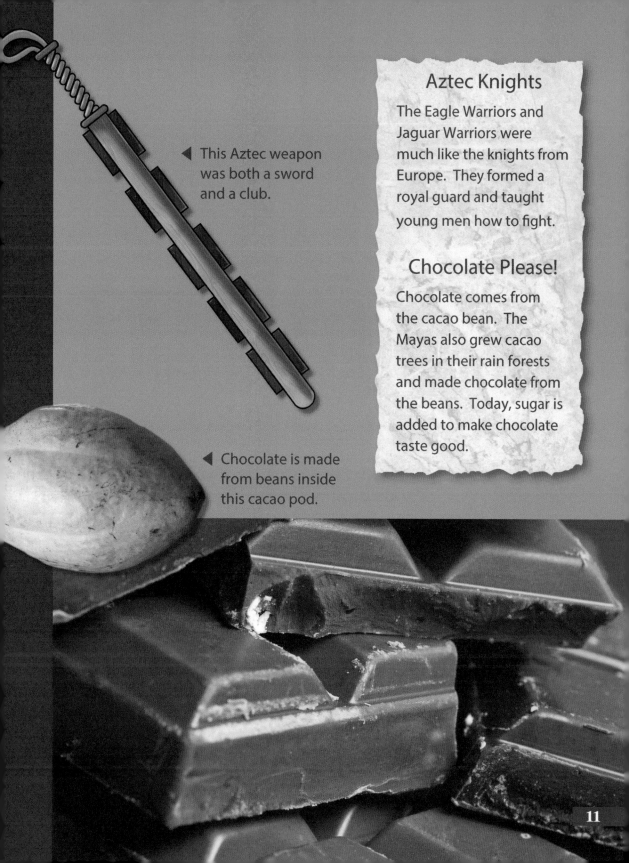

◀ This Aztec weapon was both a sword and a club.

Aztec Knights

The Eagle Warriors and Jaguar Warriors were much like the knights from Europe. They formed a royal guard and taught young men how to fight.

Chocolate Please!

Chocolate comes from the cacao bean. The Mayas also grew cacao trees in their rain forests and made chocolate from the beans. Today, sugar is added to make chocolate taste good.

◀ Chocolate is made from beans inside this cacao pod.

How to Be a Ruler

The Aztecs divided their city into different sections. Each section had a leader who served on a council. The council chose one leader. He became their ruler. He was called the Great Speaker. In 1502, the council chose Moctezuma. He was just 35 years old at the time.

Even though Moctezuma knew how to fight, most people thought of him as a thinker. He was very smart and valued learning. Moctezuma was a strict leader. He made sure everyone followed the laws. Moctezuma was not weak. He was even tough on his own family. At times, he went to the court in a disguise to see how the judges ruled. If they did not follow the law, he punished them.

▲ As a leader, Moctezuma held talks with other leaders.

Ruling Millions

Moctezuma ruled 10 million people during his reign. That's more people than live in New York City!

Reluctant Leader

Moctezuma did not want to be the Great Speaker. The council searched all over to find him. When they finally did, he was cleaning a temple.

▲ The Great Speaker Moctezuma meets with the council.

Touring Tenochtitlan

The Aztecs had lived on an island since 1325. Their city was called Tenochtitlan (tay-noch-teet-LAWN). When they found Tenochtitlan, they knew it was just right for them. A **prophecy** (PRAWF-uh-see) told them to look for an eagle eating a snake. The eagle would be perched on a cactus in the middle of swampy land. That exact place was where they should construct their great city. When they found an eagle eating a snake, the Aztecs started building.

By Moctezuma's reign, the Aztecs had built temples, ball courts, and palaces. They made floating gardens where they grew crops of corn, beans, and chilies.

To get around their city, they rode in canoes. They also built highways that went over the water to the shore. If they were being attacked, the Aztecs could pull the highways away from shore. This kept their city safe from enemies.

▼ The floating gardens are shown on the left of this picture.

▲ Venice, Italy, today

Tenochtitlan and Venice

Some people today compare Tenochtitlan to Venice, Italy. In Venice, people travel by water like they did in Tenochtitlan.

Moctezuma's Palace

Today, there are government buildings on the site where Moctezuma's palace once stood.

Mexico's Flag

Today Mexico's flag has a picture of the prophecy told to the Aztecs.

◀ The symbol from Mexico's flag shows the prophecy.

Cortés arriving by ship

Questioning Quetzalcoatl

Who is Quetzalcoatl (ket-sawl-kuh-WAH-tl)? Quetzalcoatl was a very important god to the Aztecs.

Quetzalcoatl looked like a snake with the feathers of a green and blue quetzal (ket-SAWL) bird. Aztec stories tell how he created the world and formed humans. He helped the humans by explaining to them ways to grow corn. He made the other gods angry. So, the gods sent him away. But Quetzalcoatl promised the Aztecs he would return.

The Aztecs believed he would return. They thought he would be white with a black beard. Their calendar included dates when he might return. One of the dates happened to be during Moctezuma's reign.

Moctezuma had ruled the Aztecs for 17 years when a visitor came from the East. This visitor traveled in a "house on the water." That means he came on a ship. He wore all black, just like Quetzalcoatl did in the books. And, the visitor had a black beard and white skin. His name was Hernán Cortés (her-NAN kore-TEZ).

Quetzalcoatl ▶

Such a Coincidence!

Cortés was wearing all black because it was a religious holiday for him. He even wore a hat like one that Quetzalcoatl was pictured wearing. But, Cortés was not Quetzalcoatl.

Confused by Horses

The Aztecs had never seen horses before. They thought a soldier and a horse were one creature.

Cortés Marches to Tenochtitlan

Moctezuma believed Cortés was Quetzalcoatl. He sent him gold and jewels. He hoped that Cortés would go home. Moctezuma did not want Quetzalcoatl to take control of the Aztecs.

Moctezuma thought these gifts showed his power and wealth. He thought the gifts would scare off the visitor. The Spanish saw these gifts as bribes. It only made Cortés want to visit Tenochtitlan more.

Moctezuma did not know what to do. He wondered if he should give up or fight.

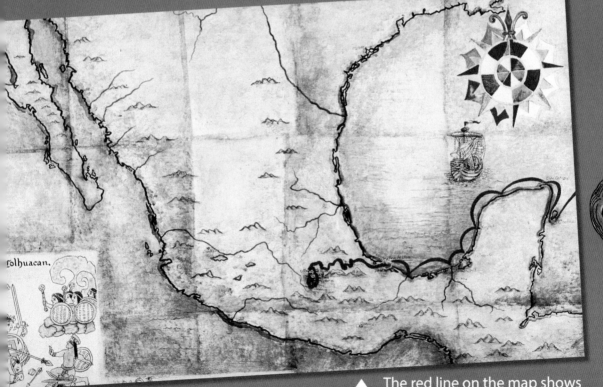

▲ The red line on the map shows the route Cortés's army took.

Cortés marched to Tenochtitlan. On the way, other tribes who did not like Moctezuma joined him. These neighboring tribes did not like the taxes they had to pay. When they saw how well the Spanish guns worked, they agreed to fight against Moctezuma.

Feathers for a King

Moctezuma also sent Cortés some quetzal feathers to show he was king. Surprisingly, the Spanish ignored the feathers. Moctezuma was probably puzzled by these actions. Quetzal feathers were very valuable to the Aztecs.

Before the March

When Moctezuma hesitated, the Spanish saw that as a sign of weakness. The Aztec army was much greater than the Spanish forces and could have defeated them once and for all.

◄ Map of Tenochtitlan

The End of the Aztecs

Cortés was amazed when he saw Tenochtitlan. He and his men marched right over the highways. Moctezuma was a good **diplomat** (DIP-luh-mat) and welcomed them. Within days, Cortés took Moctezuma captive. In the meantime, the Spanish killed some Aztec warriors. When the people became angry, Cortés sent Moctezuma to calm them down. The people threw rocks at Moctezuma. He was wounded. He died a few days later.

▼ Aztec people may have killed their great leader.

▲ The Aztecs revolted against the Spanish.

Then, a **revolt** took place that drove the Spanish out of Tenochtitlan. Cortés rebuilt his army. Then, he overtook the city once more.

Cortés did not approve of the Aztec belief in many gods. He tore down their temples and built churches in their places. The great empire that had ruled millions came to a quick end.

Revolt

In the revolt after Moctezuma's death, the Aztecs destroyed all the Spanish cannons. They also killed more than half of the Spanish army.

Conflicting Accounts of Death

The Aztecs claimed that Moctezuma died when the Spanish stabbed him. The Spanish account says that his own people killed him with stones.

Lasting Symbols

Some Aztecs took statues and symbols before Cortés got to them. They hid them in nearby towns. The symbols that survived tell people today about life as an Aztec.

Other Rulers and Their Nations

There were more great nations in the Western hemisphere near the time of the Aztecs. These leaders built cities, roads, ball courts, and bridges. The following pages tell about some amazing leaders who ruled the Incas and Mayas.

Incas Rule!

The Incas lived in the Andes (AN-deez) Mountains. Their first known leader was Manco Capac (mahng-KO kah-PAHK). The Incas called their leader the Sapa Inca. They believed he was a **descendent** (dih-SEN-duhnt) of the sun god.

▼ Andes Mountains

The Incas did not control very much land at first. That all changed when a man named Pachacuti (pah-chah-KOO-tee) came to power. He became the Sapa Inca in 1438. He led the Incan army and conquered nearby lands. Soon, he ruled nine million people. The Incan empire extended for thousands of miles.

To keep track of his people, he chose four governors. These men were in charge of others, who were in charge of others, and so on. In this way, the Sapa Inca knew what was happening in his empire.

Where Are the Incas?

The Incas lived in what is modern-day Peru and Chile.

Keeping Track

The Incas kept track of wealth and supplies by using a set of strings called a *quipu* (KEY-poo). Today, historians still work to understand these mysterious strings.

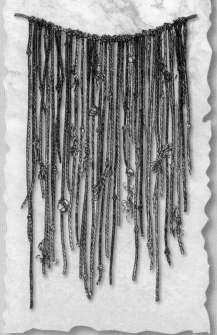

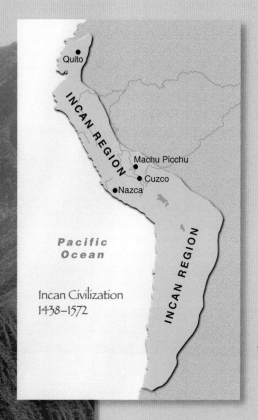

Incan Civilization 1438–1572

◀ Map showing Incan empire

Other Rulers and Their Nations

Atahualpa

The End of the Incan Rulers

In 1531, the Spanish landed ships near the Incas. The explorers brought sickness with them. The new Sapa Inca became very sick. Before his death, he chose a son to be the next emperor. But that son also died. So, the Sapa Inca decided to divide his kingdom. His other two sons each got part. One son, Atahualpa (aw-tuh-WAWL-puh), ruled the North. The other son, Huáscar (WAHS-kawr), ruled the South.

The brothers fought for control of the land. Atahualpa won, but the war weakened him. That is when the Spanish moved in. They captured Atahualpa. The Spanish demanded that the people send gold. If they received enough, they promised to let the leader go free.

The Incas did not realize that the Spanish were lying. In the end, the Spanish killed Atahualpa. The Incan empire quickly came to an end.

▼ Machu Picchu

Deadly Diseases

One of the diseases the Spanish brought with them was smallpox. Today, there are vaccinations to protect people from this disease.

Machu Picchu

The Spanish never found the city of Machu Picchu (MAW-choo PEE-choo). In 1911, an American found the city. It is high up on a mountain cliff. Today, visitors can hike there and see the Incan ruins.

Francisco Pizarro

Francisco Pizarro (puh-ZAWR-oh) was the Spanish leader who defeated the Incas.

Other Rulers and Their Nations

My, Oh Maya!

The Mayan people lived in **city-states**. Each city-state had a ruling family. Mayan priests helped these families rule.

Kings created **steles** (STEE-leez). Steles were stone columns. Glyphs were written on these. Most of the time, steles were used to brag about a king. The glyphs described the greatness of the king and all the things he did. Mayan kings even carved glyphs on temple stairways.

Most of the Mayan kings had interesting names. How would you feel if you had the name Skull II, Shield Jaguar, or Green Sun Turtle Tooth?

◀ Mayan stele found in Central America

▲ This is Catherwood's drawing of Tulum.

In 2005, the TV show "Survivor" was filmed where the Mayas once lived. These ruins are on the Yucatán Peninsula.

Two Explorers

In the 1800s, John Stephens and Frederick Catherwood explored where the Mayas had lived. Stephens wrote a book. Catherwood drew pictures of the area. This was how others learned about the Mayan ruins.

Mayan Almanacs

Mayan calendars were like **almanacs** (AL-muh-naks). Today, farmers' almanacs give predictions for the coming year.

The Mayas kept track of time using two calendars. One helped them name their children and find the unlucky days. The other kept track of the movements of the stars. They used this second calendar to plan their lives.

Mayan calendar ▶

Other Rulers and Their Nations

Mayan Talents

To show that their city was great, Mayan kings built great buildings. The kings lived in grand palaces and built huge pyramids. The pyramids stood 10 stories high. The tops of the pyramids were flat. On the flat tops, were temples. They worshipped Mayan gods here. Most temples honored the gods of nature. Amazingly, they built all this without metal tools!

The Mayas played the first team sport in history. They played this ball game with a rubber ball. The ball was bounced off their bodies.

The Mayas were also skilled farmers. They rotated crops to keep the dirt rich. **Terraces** (TAIR-ruhs-es) helped them farm on sloping hillsides. Mayan kings looked to their gods to provide rain and sunshine for these crops.

◀ Farming terraces

▲ Mayan ball court

Rubber from the Mayas

Rubber balls are still used in many sports games today.

Sports in the West

The Aztecs played a ball game similar to the Mayan game. One Aztec town had 11 ball courts!

How to Make Rubber

Rubber is taken from the sap of a tree in the rain forest. This rubber makes the balls bouncy.

In many ways, the Aztec, Mayan, and Incan rulers were great. Moctezuma is just one example of these remarkable rulers. They knew how to govern people and extend their empires. They also built grand cities. In time, people will discover more ruins and learn more stories about these amazing **civilizations** (siv-uh-luh-ZAY-shuhnz).

Glossary

almanacs—books that help make predictions about things like weather and crops

astronomy—the study of the movements of the sky

cacao—beans that are used to make cocoa and chocolate

city-states—ancient cities that ruled themselves independently

civilizations—societies that have writing and keep track of records

descendent—relative of someone from the past

diplomat—someone who deals with other civilizations or nations

glyphs—picture writing; hieroglyphics

prophecy—something described before it happens

quipu—set of strings used by the Incas to record information about the empire

reign—the time period that a person rules

revolt—when common people fight against their leaders

rituals—certain ceremonies performed by religious leaders

sacrifices—gifts offered to the gods; sometimes human beings were killed

steles—stone monuments with writing on them

terraces—areas of flat land on sloping hillsides used for farming

Index

Image Credits

Printed in Poland
by Amazon Fulfillment
Poland Sp. z o.o., Wrocław